FESTIVE

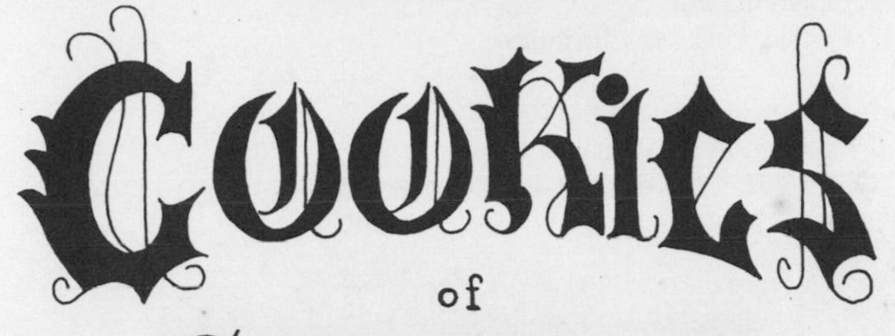

of

CHRISTMAS

Norma Jost Voth

Illustrated by Ellen Jane Price

HERALD PRESS
Scottdale, Pennsylvania
Waterloo, Ontario

Library of Congress Cataloging in Publication Data

Voth, Norma Jost.
Festive cookies of Christmas.

1. Cookies. 2. Christmas cookery.
3. Cookery, International. I. Title.
TX772.V67 641.8'654 81-18258
ISBN 0-8361-1983-5 AACR2

FESTIVE COOKIES OF CHRISTMAS

Library of Congress Catalog Card Number: 81-18258
International Standard Book Number: 0-8361-1983-5
Printed in the United States of America

96 95 94 93 92 91 10 9 8 7 6

To my dear sister and her daughter—
Yvonne and Laura Dunn—who love to
bake cookies together

Special thanks to cookie enthusiasts Liz Spears, Anne Hyrne, Adaline Karber, Mary Koyama, and Virginia Sharp for testing recipes; to Ruth Capper, Helen Epp, LaDonna Bontrager (Amish); Catherine Weidner (Moravians); the Austrian Consulate of New York City; Marthe Nussbaumer (Alsace); Ester Harvest and Johanna Reynolds (Denmark); Terttu Gilbert (Finland); Doris Walter and Magdalena Meyer (Germany); Aristea Pettis (Greece); Johanna Hekkert and Jan Gleysteen (Holland); Jeannie Bertucelli Snyder, Edith Bertucelli, and Matilde Oliverio (Italy); Rosa Calvillo and Elma Voth (Mexico); Vera Kawulka (Poland); Dr. Ingrid Gamstorp, Margaret Carlsen, and Brigetta Kellgrin (Sweden), Doreen Leith (Scotland); and Lily Gyger (Switzerland), for helpful contributions.

"Finally, it was Christmas Eve. At dinner everybody tried to pretend nothing was particularly special. But everything was. The food tasted more delicious, the air smelled fresher, sweeter; sounds came at a higher pitch; sights seemed sharper, colors richer. It was the same house we lived in all those other 364 evenings, the same rooms, the same furniture, the same stairs, the same people, and yet they seemed now somehow different, transformed."

—Philip Kundhart, Jr., *My Father's House* (New York: Random House).

Of Lebkuchen, Springerle, and Ammonia Cookies

In my childhood home, mother had a few of her own special cookie recipes which she quietly and courageously baked every Christmas despite the fact that her daughters thought them quite dull.

These old recipes for *Lebkuchen*, *Springerle* (pages 40 and 48), and Ammonia Cookies, gathered from Canadian friends, were penned into a handwritten cookbook with fond memories of visits and warm hospitality.

Mom packed her yearly cookie cache high on a cupboard shelf. But she need not have. Not once did we disturb that box. We much preferred to pilfer gumdrop peppernuts and peanut brittle.

Only in recent years have I discovered, with much chagrin, the lovely delicacy of those Old World cookies—the soft, chewy texture of *Lebkuchen*, the gentle hint of anise in *Springerle*, and experimented with that old-fashioned leavening of our grandmothers, bakers' ammonia.

And wouldn't you know! When I offer these gems at Christmas, my son, with that same maddening aloofness, passes over my discovery for everyday chocolate chip cookies and fudge brownies. Guess who's chuckling now!

Moravian Christmas Cookies

"My mother, Lula Brandon, gave me this recipe (p. 8) which I am sure came from her mother," writes Catherine Weidner, of Bethlehem, Pennsylvania. "Every year mother made up the dough just after Thanksgiving. Baking day was great fun for the whole family and was often done in the early evening so everyone could help.

"Mother took a small lump of dough and rolled and rolled to get it as thin as possible. My four sisters and I each had a job—placing cookies on a tin, watching the oven, removing the baked cookies to cool, stacking cookies by shape in big lard tins to store until Christmas. . . . The aroma was wonderful. Mother made these cookies every year until she died at 89.

"Moravian cutters, handed down from mother to daughter, come in all shapes and sizes—stars, angels, trees, leaves, hearts, bells, candles, boys, girls, animals, or birds. Some are so tiny they are hardly a bite. I prize highly those from my mother."

Antique Moravian cutters can be found in the Moravian museum in Bethlehem. A few patterns appear on page 9.

Organist, musician, and pastor's wife, Catherine Weidner enjoys a full schedule of church work and entertaining in her home.

Mrs. Henry Brandon's Moravian Christmas Cookies

Mrs. Brandon's daughters bake these cookies by the hundreds for their families and grandchildren. The recipe is much in demand for its lovely combination of molasses and spices, complemented by the subtle flavor of orange. The dough can be rolled to "tissue paper thin."

- 1 cup dark molasses
- 1⅓ cups brown sugar, packed
- ¼ cup + 2 tbsp. lard or shortening
- 1½ tsp. soda
- 2 tbsp hot water
- 1 tbsp. orange extract
- ½ tsp. ginger
- ½ tsp. cinnamon
- ½ tsp. cloves
- ½ tsp. mace
- 4-5 cups flour

Combine molasses, sugar, lard, and soda dissolved in 2 tbsp. hot water over low heat. Melt and cool. Add orange extract. Gradually add flour sifted with spices. Dough should be firm. Mix and knead thoroughly. Cover well and set in cool place to ripen.

Roll small amounts of dough to paper thinness on well-floured, cloth-covered board. Cut into shapes with floured cutters. Place on greased tins, smoothing out any air bubbles. Bake at 350° until light brown. Watch carefully. Store in airtight container.

(Mrs. Brandon used "Puerto Rico Molasses." She also used lard in the dough which makes the cookies flaky and crisp.)

Old Cookie Cutters

Some of the finest early cookie cutters were produced in the Pennsylvania Dutch country where bright colors, ornamentation, and good food inspired the tinsmith.

Designs came from the tinworker's surroundings and he turned out patterns of horses, birds, stars, flowers, hearts, among many others. Cutters were shaped from freehand drawings and frequently were made just before holidays. Many families had one member who could turn out their patterns.

Early cutters were usually made of strong, thin steel plate generously coated with tin. The older the cutter, the deeper the cutting edge. Holes were stamped in the back to allow air to escape when the cutter was pressed into the dough.

Antique cutters were often signed by the tinsmith, dated, and numbered. Recently one rare cutter, nearly a hundred years old, sold for $1,025 at an auction!

A few craftsmen who are reviving this old art and handcraft, sign, date, and number their cutters just as the old tinsmiths did earlier.

Old-Fashioned Sugar Cookies

"My rolled cookie recipe comes from a small bakery run by a Slavic lady who was a friend of our family. I have done almost everything with the dough but walk on it and never had a failure!" says Ruth Capper, Dellroy, Ohio. Here is a trusty recipe to cut into stars, trees, and bells for children to decorate.

1 cup butter
1 cup sugar
2 eggs
1½ tsp. vanilla
½ tsp. soda
1 tsp. baking powder
½ tsp. salt
1 tsp. nutmeg (optional)
3-3½ cups flour

In a mixing bowl, beat butter until creamy. Beat in sugar, eggs, and vanilla, mixing well. Sift dry ingredients and gradually add to creamed mixture. Beat well. Cover and chill overnight. Roll out dough to ⅛-inch thickness on well-floured board. Cut into favorite designs.

Place on greased baking sheet and bake at 350° for 5-7 minutes or until lightly browned. Cool immediately on racks. Decorate as desired. Makes about 4 dozen cookies.

"I remember my grandmother baking big molasses cookies in her grassburner oven," says Helen Epp, author of *A Treasury of Cookie Recipes.* "She made a fire with bundles of prairie grass. When it had burned down and the coals were just right, she put the cookies on black pans that were exactly the width of the oven. How she knew when the temperature was right, I don't know.

"Grandmother used her own homemade molasses and flour ground from their own wheat. How we loved the smell of those cookies. That was my first lesson in cookie baking."

For the Love of a Cookie!

Ruth Capper has collected cookie cutters for years. But it's not only the cutters Ruth likes, it's the cookie baking as well—especially for her favorite project, the annual Dellroy Historical Society Festival.

During this three-day gala, Ruth and several helpers bake about 3,000 gingerbread boys from an old family recipe. She bakes nonstop from 8:00 in the morning to 6:00 in the evening "on an old stove like mother's, so our cookies are very homemade.

"It's so interesting to see grown men stand in line just to get a warm cookie," says Ruth. "Several remarked they had never eaten a gingerbread boy before and surely never one that had been baked before their own eyes.

"We didn't always have time to decorate the cookies, and one little boy stood a long time looking at his plain cookie. He finally asked, 'Where are the eyes?' When I told him the boy was asleep, he seemed satisfied."

Ruth Capper is president of the national Cookie Cutter Collector's Club. (Yes, there really is such an organization!) She works as secretary, loves gardening, baking, and her role of busy farmer's wife as well.

Chocolate-Covered Pretzels

In the Amish/Mennonite community of Yoder, Kansas, LaDonna Bontrager is known for the good, country-style food she serves in her little *Koffa Haus* (coffeehouse). At Christmas she is lauded for the gallons of peppernuts, cookies, and chocolate-covered pretzels she turns out in her large farm home kitchen. Big trays of these goodies are served to family and friends throughout the holiday season.

Place 6 oz. *coating chocolate* or semi-sweet chocolate chips in top of double boiler over hot, not boiling, water. Add 1 tbsp. shortening or *paramount crystals* (see Shopper's Guide, p. 100). Stir until mixture begins to melt. Remove from heat and stir until completely melted. Coatings dip best at 85°. Dip each pretzel in coating.

Remove with tongs and lay on baking sheets lined with waxed paper. Chill, uncovered, until coating is set. Stack and store in airtight containers. Makes 4-5 dozen.

To achieve professional-looking results, use dark or white *coating chocolate*, which is available in some cake decorating and candy stores or at candy counters in some department stores.

Cherry Chocolate Chippers

For the chocolate chip cookie lover, here is the ultimate Christmas combination enhanced by maraschino cherries.

- ¾ cup margarine
- 1 cup brown sugar
- 1 egg
- 1 tsp. vanilla
- 2¼ cups flour
- 1 tsp. baking powder
- ½ tsp. salt
- 6 oz. semi-sweet chocolate chips
- ½ cup chopped nuts
- ½ cup shredded coconut (optional)
- ½ cup chopped maraschino cherries

Cream sugar and margarine until light and fluffy. Add egg and vanilla and beat well. Gradually add flour sifted with baking powder and salt. Mix thoroughly. Gradually add chocolate, nuts, coconut (optional), and then carefully fold in the cherries. Mix lightly. Drop by spoonfuls onto ungreased baking sheet. Bake at 350° for 10-12 minutes. Makes about 12 dozen.

CHRISTMAS at Grandmother Jost's meant dozens of cousins filling that big white frame house at the end of Main Street in Hillsboro. It was a day of laughter, giggling, and games of hide and seek. At dinner, we cousins sat crammed elbow to elbow, at the long oak table in the kitchen, eating ham, *Zwieback*, *Pluma Moos*, and grandma's spicy, hard peppernuts.

However, the fun ended abruptly when one of the aunts marshaled us into the living room to perform. Who can forget that room with its slightly stuffy smell (it wasn't heated every day) and grandparents sitting primly in front of the bay window, bright with white lace curtains, a flowering Christmas cactus, and spindly geraniums in tin cans. Aunts and uncles sat in straight-back chairs around the room.

We children stood in a line, slightly embarrassed, trying not to giggle, and looking hard at the floor while taking turns reciting the verses we had learned at church. Uncles and aunts nodded, smiling approval. Grandmother more than rewarded our sing-song efforts with little gifts and sacks of nuts and candy. Grandfather gave us each a dime. Those were Christmases with roots, and family, and memories.

We always knew Christmas was coming when mother got out our book of *Wünschen* (wishes). The cover had a pale pastel design, tied with bright yarn. Poems and verses, all handwritten, filled the book. There were shorter poems for the littler children and longer ones for those who were older. I remember some with six or seven verses. These we memorized to recite two or three times—first on Christmas morning for our parents and then again for grandparents at family gatherings. *(Bertha Fast Harder, Elkhart, Indiana)*

Helen Epp recalls learning these Christmas poems for her country school programs. "Sometimes you learned more than one," she says. "The longer the poems, the more you could say and recite, the smarter you were!"

Stained-Glass Windows

A cookie as pretty as a picture—and good to eat, too. The colorful stained-glass effect is easily achieved with hard colored candies.

Eugene Valasek, Canton, Ohio, designed and crafted a special cutter for this cookie for the 1980 Cookie Cutter Collector's Convention.

½ cup sugar	2 cups flour
⅓ cup margarine	2 tbsp. milk
1 egg	10-12 rolls candy, assorted colors
½ tsp. vanilla	large silver dragées
¼ tsp. salt	¼ cup light corn syrup
1 tsp. baking powder	

Cream sugar and margarine until light and fluffy; beat in egg, vanilla, and salt. Gradually add flour sifted with baking powder. Alternate with milk. Chill overnight or until dough handles easily.

Flour pastry cloth or board and rolling pin. Roll out small amounts of dough to ⅛-inch thickness. Dip special stained-glass cutter (see Shopper's Guide, p. 101) in flour, cut dough, and gently ease cookie onto foil-lined cookie sheet. Tap lightly until dough drops out. With toothpick or pointed object, gently lift out cutouts, including hanging holes.

Outline each triangle with about 15 dragées. Break candies (Lifesavers) in half. Into each star cutout place ½ piece yellow candy, into each heart ½ piece red candy, into each triangle ½ piece green candy. (Triangles are not quite as large; you may need a little less, as candy may cook over.) You may also need to substitute colors.

Bake at 350° for 5-7 minutes, until all candies are melted. Watch closely. Cool *completely* on cookie sheet on wire rack. *Peel* foil from cookies. Repeat with remaining cookies. Makes about 1 dozen. (Small cutouts baked separately make delightful refreshments for a dolls' tea party.) Bring corn syrup to boiling over medium heat for 2 minutes. Brush corn syrup evenly over each cookie.

Adaline Karber, San Jose, California, baked enough of these cookies to decorate a Christmas tree for her church.

Lacy Pecan Wafers

Blending flavors of carmel and pecan, these candy-like cookies go well with ice cream or may be filled with whipped cream for an elegant dessert.

- ⅔ cup ground pecans
- ⅓ cup sugar
- ½ cup butter
- 1 tbsp. flour
- 2 tbsp. milk
- ½ tsp. vanilla

Combine all ingredients in a skillet over medium heat and cook until blended. Keep warm. Drop batter (it will be thin) by teaspoonfuls about 3 inches apart, on well-greased sheet. Allow only 4 or 6 cookies to each pan. Bake at 350° for 5 minutes. Cool on baking sheet 1 minute. Working quickly, remove cookie with spatula, turn over and curl around handle of wooden spoon.

If cookies become brittle, return to oven 1 minute to soften. Cool. Store in airtight container or they may become soft. Makes about 32.

Meringue Kisses

This easy cookie makes an attractive addition to a Christmas gift box or cookie tray.

2 egg whites
¾ cup powdered sugar

6 oz. mini chocolate chips
or ½ cup chopped nuts (walnuts, pecans, or filberts)

Bring egg whites to room temperature. Beat egg whites until foamy. Continue beating while adding sifted sugar gradually. Beat until very stiff. Fold in chocolate bits or nuts. Drop by rounded teaspoonfuls onto parchment-lined cookie sheet. Place in 350° oven and turn off heat immediately. Without opening the door, leave the meringues in oven for at least 6 hours or overnight.

Store in airtight container. Add to cookie gift boxes at the last minute as meringues do not keep well. This recipe makes 2½-3 dozen.

Adaline Karber's Pecan Crisps

Adaline Karber loves to bake—cookies, cakes, breads—with wedding cakes and catering receptions her specialty. While testing recipes for this book, she created an original of her own—Pecan Crisps—a delicate light cookie with the continental flavoring of orange flower water.

½ cup sweet butter
2 tbsp. sugar
1½ cups cake flour
1 tsp. orange flower water* or 2 tsp. vanilla
¾ cup chopped pecans

Beat butter and sugar until creamy. Add orange flower water. Gradually add sifted cake flour and beat well. Gently mix in nuts; do not overbeat. Roll dough into balls smaller than a walnut and place on parchment-lined baking pan. Press balls down very lightly with a water glass. Bake at 300° for 15 minutes. Cookies should be firm but not brown. Makes 2½ dozen.

---

*Used frequently in France and the Middle East, *orange flower water* is made from the blossom of Alpine French Riviera Bitter Orange trees. Its delicate flavor enhances cakes, pastries, cream, crepes, candies, and waffles. (Strength and quality may vary.)

Alsatian Schokolade Kugeln
(Chocolate Balls)

Rich and chocolatey, crusty on the outside, soft and moist inside—these chocolate balls are a tradition in Marthe Nussbaumer's French/Alsatian kitchen.

- 2 eggs
- ½ cup + 3 tbsp. sugar
- 4 oz. unsweetened chocolate, grated
- ½ tsp. cinnamon
- 1 tsp. vanilla
- 5 tbsp. + 1 tsp. flour
- 2 cups + 6 tbsp. ground almonds
- Powdered sugar

Beat eggs and sugar until light and fluffy. Add remaining ingredients and beat well. Pat into a ball and chill in refrigerator at least 1 hour. With a teaspoon, spoon out small balls of dough about ¾ inch in diameter. Roll each in sifted, powdered sugar.

Place on greased baking sheet and allow to dry 4-5 hours in warm kitchen. Bake at 475° for 3-5 minutes. Cool 10 minutes on baking pan and remove to cooling racks. Balls will have light outer crust and soft centers. Makes about 60 balls.

Marthe Nussbaumer's Dukatentaler

Tasty French, Alsatian, and Swiss baking all blend in Marthe Nussbaumer's large farm kitchen near Altkirch (Alsace), France. *Dukatentaler* are from her Christmas collection.

- ½ cup + 1½ tsp. sweet butter
- ½ cup sugar
- 2 eggs
- 1 tsp. vanilla or ½ tsp. vanilla sugar
- 2 cups + 3 tbsp. flour
- ¼ tsp. baking powder
- Chocolate Filling
- Chocolate Glaze

Beat butter until creamy. Beat in sugar, eggs, and vanilla. Add flour sifted with baking powder to cream mixture. Knead until light and shiny. Chill overnight. Roll to ¼-inch thickness on well-floured board. Cut in dollar-sized circles and place on greased baking sheet. Bake at 350° for about 5 minutes or until lightly browned. Cool on wire racks.

Spread half the circles with Chocolate Filling. Cover with top circle. Glaze ½ of top circle of each cookie with Chocolate Glaze. Makes about 5 dozen double cookies.

Chocolate Filling: 4 tbsp. butter, ½ cup powdered sugar, 1 tsp. vanilla, 1 egg yolk, beaten, 2 oz. unsweetened chocolate,

melted. Cream butter. Beat in sugar, vanilla, and egg yolk. Melt chocolate over double boiler and add to mixture. Beat until smooth.
Chocolate Glaze: Mix together ½ cup powdered sugar, 2 tbsp. cocoa, 5 tsp. boiling water, ¼ tsp. vanilla.

A duke in Venice once owned a mint where they made Dukats, *coins named after the owner.*

Originating in Bohemia, the Taler *was minted in* Joachimstal *(Joachim's Valley), and the coin took on the name of* Joachimstaler. *Our English word, dollar, comes from the German* Taler.

Someone, somewhere along the way combined these two words to name this buttery, dollar-sized cookie with a rich chocolate filling. It, too, may be worth its weight in gold.

Family Secrets

In Austrian homes, Christmas begins the Saturday before Advent. In the household of Baroness Maria Von Trapp (whose story was told in "The Sound of Music"), the whole family trooped out to the woods to gather fresh evergreen boughs for their Advent wreath. Around the warmth of a crackling fire in the living room, they tied the fresh, fragrant branches onto a large old wagon wheel. Four white candles, one for each week of Advent, were added. Then the big wreath was hung from the ceiling, suspended by four strong red ribbons.

After supper came time for festive ceremony—lighting the first candle, singing, and prayers. Mrs. Von Trapp brought out a bowlful of cards on which were written the names of the different members of the household. In greatest secrecy, each drew a name and then tossed the card into the fire. From that moment until Christmas, each person had another "in his special care," doing as many little favors and services as possible for that person.

This lovely old custom created a real atmosphere of helpfulness, charity, and true Christmas spirit, remembers Baroness Von Trapp. (Adapted from "Christmas with the Trapp Family," by Greta Sciutto and Margaret Thompson, *In the Very Name of Christmas* [Boston: Chapman & Grimes, Inc.].)

Austrian Vanille Kipferl

(Vanilla Crescents)

One bite calls for another of these butter-rich cookies dipped in vanilla sugar.

- 1 cup butter
- ½ cup sugar
- 2 egg yolks
- 3 cups flour
- 1 cup ground blanched almonds
- ½ cup vanilla sugar

Cream butter and sugar until light and fluffy. Add egg yolks and beat well. Add sifted flour, ½ cup at a time. Add almonds and continue beating. Refrigerate—not more than 1 hour.

Roll into pencil-thin strips. Cut in 3-inch lengths; turn ends to form crescent. (For consistent shapes, the *Kipferl* may be shaped around a glass or bottle.) Place on lightly greased baking sheet. Bake at 350° for 12-15 minutes or until golden brown. Roll in vanilla sugar mixture. Store in airtight container.

Vanilla sugar is made by placing a vanilla bean or empty vanilla bean pod in a closed jar with sugar for 2-3 days.

Austrian Hussar Rounds

Hussar (*hoo*-zahr) was the name given to the elite division of the Hungarian light cavalry of the 15th century. *Rounds* may refer to their ammunition or bullets. But cookies by this name are quite the opposite—soft, buttery, and light!

1 cup softened butter
½ cup + 2 tbsp. sugar
2 tbsp. grated lemon peel
½ tsp. vanilla
3 egg yolks, beaten
3-3½ cups flour
1 egg white
Coarsely chopped blanched almonds
Apricot jam
Powdered sugar

Cream butter and sugar until fluffy; add lemon peel and vanilla. Add egg yolks alternately with spoons of flour. Mix well. Work in remaining flour until dough is firm and smooth. Pinch off small pieces of dough and roll into 1-inch balls. Make indentations on top of each cookie. Brush with egg white beaten with 1 tbsp. water. Roll each cookie in almonds.

Place on greased baking sheet. Bake at 350° 20-25 minutes or until delicately browned. Cool. Before serving place dab of apricot jam in center. Serve dusted with powdered sugar. Makes about 4 dozen.

Austrian Ischler Tartlets

A seductive flavor duo of almonds and raspberries will call for more than seconds. *Ischler Tartlets* originate in the area of Bad Ischl.

2 cups flour
1 cup ground blanched almonds
1 cup sweet butter
½ cup sugar
Raspberry jam
Chocolate Glaze
Blanched almond halves

Combine flour and ground almonds in a bowl; work in butter as for pie dough. Blend in sugar. Knead until smooth and dough holds together well. Chill. Roll small portions of dough to ⅛-inch thickness between sheets of waxed paper. Cut with 2-2½-inch round biscuit cutter.

Place on greased baking sheet and bake at 350° for 8-10 minutes or until light golden in color. Remove to racks and cool. When ready to serve, place cookies together in pairs with jam in center. Frost top cookie with Chocolate Glaze. Top with almond half.

Chocolate Glaze: Melt 4 oz. semi-sweet chocolate and 1 tbsp. butter over low heat; beat until smooth. Spread tops of cookies.

Austrian Coconut Macaroons

A hint of fresh lemon makes this a special treat.

- 2-⅔ cups fresh coconut, peeled and shredded*
- 1 cup sugar
- 1 egg white
- 1 tbsp. grated lemon peel
- 2 tbsp. lemon juice, strained
- 3 egg whites
- 3 tbsp. flour

Combine coconut, sugar, 1 egg white, lemon peel, and lemon juice in medium saucepan, stirring over low heat until luke warm. Remove from heat and cool. Beat remaining egg whites until they form soft peaks. Gradually fold egg whites into cooled coconut mixture. Add flour gradually and combine gently.

Place heaping teaspoons of mixture at 1½-inch intervals on well-greased baking sheet. Bake at 275° for about 20-25 minutes or until golden brown. Makes 3 dozen.

---

*You may substitute commercial coconut.

Linzer Tartlets

Reminiscent of Linzer torte, these special cookies combine filberts, raspberries, and a chocolate glaze for a marvelous flavor treat.

½ cup flour
½ cup sifted bread or cake crumbs
⅔ cup ground filberts
⅔ cup butter
⅓ cup sugar
2 tbsp. unsweetened chocolate, grated
Raspberry jam
Chocolate Glaze

Combine flour, crumbs, and filberts in a bowl; work in butter. Blend in sugar and chocolate. Knead dough until it holds together. Chill. On floured board, roll small portions of dough to ⅛-inch thickness. (Dough may be slightly crumbly.) With 2-inch biscuit cutter, cut in circles and place on ungreased baking sheet. Bake at 325° for 10-12 minutes or until cookies are firm. Cool on wire racks.

Before serving, place cookies together in pairs with jam in center. (Apricot jam is a good alternate.) Ice with Chocolate Glaze, p. 25.) Makes about 1½ dozen double cookies.

A Dutch Saint Nicholas Eve Party

CHOCOLADE LETTER (Chocolate Letters)

SPECULAAS (Cookies)

SPRITS (Letter Cookies)

PEPERNOTEN (Peppernut Cookies)

MARSEPEIN (Marzipan)

BORSTPLAAT (Sugar Candies)

CHOCOLADE MELK (Hot Chocolate)

BANKETLETTER (Saint Nicholas Letter)

ST. NICHOLAS DAY in Holland (December 6) in a time of great fun and merriment for all. "Excitement begins to build as soon as the good saint arrives in town, usually a few days early," recalls Johanna Hekkert of her childhood in the Netherlands. "As soon as he is known to be around, the children set out their shoes at night with treats for his horse, hoping for a small present in return. In the morning, on the way to school, they love to brag about what Sinterklaas left for them."

The big evening is December 5 when the whole family and their closest friends gather to welcome a visit from St. Nicholas. "Suddenly there is a loud knock at the door and a black hand reaches in, tossing *Pepernoten* (tiny cookies) across the floor. That's *Swarte Piet* (Black Peter), his helper, who accompanies him everywhere. The children scramble to see who can pick up the most cookies," says Johanna.

Then the father, or the head of the house, invites St. Nicholas into the living room, asking him to sit in the best chair. The children stand around, looking up at this stately man in his long robe and bishop's miter, listening anxiously as he reads from a book in which everyone's good and bad deeds are recorded. Good children get presents, of course, and for those who need improvement, *Swarte Piet* has a birch switch to encourage better behavior.

"In our home we always exchanged surprises on this evening. Gifts were disguised to make the final discovery more delightful. A small box might be wrapped many times inside a huge unwieldy box, or little things were hidden inside a vegetable or in the pudding. Clues written in poetry often led to a big box somewhere in the cellar. Or perhaps the doorbell rang and there was a present on the steps outside, but there was no one in sight.

"When all the gifts were opened and the poems read, mother served *Speculaas* and hot chocolate. We each got our initials in solid chocolate—mine was a *J*. Often dad would buy a *Banketletter* (cake in the shape of a letter), one for my mother in the letter *M* (for mother), or at times mother would order one from the bakery in the shape of a *B* (for van den Boom, our family name).

"On Christmas there were no presents. It is a religious day, set aside for church and family gatherings. If Christmas happened to fall on Monday, we went to the two regular church services on Sunday, then twice on Monday (Christmas Day) and again twice on the Second Day of Christmas (Tuesday). That was a lot of church!"

Dutch Speculaas

Crunchy *Speculaas* cookies were traditionally shaped in elaborately carved molds, but are just as delicious cut in squares sprinkled with almonds. In Holland, St. Nicholas rewards good children with *Speculaas*, *Pepernoten* (peppernut cookies), and *Tai Tai* (a gingerbread-like cookie).

- ½ cup butter or margarine
- 1 cup brown sugar
- 1 egg
- 2 tbsp. milk
- 2½ cups flour
- ½ tsp. baking powder
- ½ tsp. salt
- 1 tsp. cinnamon
- ½ tsp. cloves
- ½ tsp. nutmeg
- ⅛ tsp. cardamom
- ½ cup sliced almonds

Cream butter and sugar until fluffy. Add egg and milk. Beat well. Sift together dry ingredients and blend slowly into creamed mixture. Chill overnight.

For Squares or Cookie Cutters: Roll well-chilled dough on floured board. Cut with floured cutter or cut in squares or rectangles with knife. Place on greased baking sheet. Sprinkle with sliced almonds. Bake at 300° for 12-15 minutes or until edges start to brown. Cool on racks. Store in airtight container.

For Molded Cookies: Chill dough in freezer 15 minutes. Generously flour inside of mold. On well-floured board, roll dough thick enough to fill inside of mold. Cut piece of dough to fit in mold and press in. Flatten with floured rolling pin. Slide spatula across to remove excess dough. Remove immediately by turning mold over and tapping on back. Ease cookie onto greased baking sheet.

For large mold, lay greased sheet on mold, invert to release cookie. Bake at 300° about 20 minutes or until edges begin to brown. Cool. Store in airtight container. Makes 1½ dozen.

Ans van den Hoogen, a professional baker, says *Speculaas* retain clearer details of the mold when dough is very stiff and less baking powder is used. Baker van den Hoogen allows, however, "In our shop we go more for flavor and are not so concerned with shape."

Johanna Hekkert, Sunnyvale, California, collects old Speculaas *molds, some of which are two to three feet high, and uses them as wall decorations. She also celebrates St. Nicholas Day with her children by filling their shoes with small gifts and baking large batches of this St. Nicholas Day treat.*

The Famous Honey Cakes of Nürnberg

Long before there was sugar, monks in the monastery kitchens near Nürnberg, Germany, were baking *Lebkuchen* from honey that was brought to them by beekeepers in the nearby Lorenz Forest.

At that time baking powder was unknown, too, so honey became the leavening agent. Mixed with flour, it was left to ferment several months, which gave the dough its lifting power and the famous *Lebkuchen* flavor as well. Fourth-century honey cakes were simply made of flour, honey, and spices.

After Nürnberg was settled, a trade route opened to Venice in the 14th century, making available ginger, cinnamon, nutmeg, anise, almonds, rosewater, citron, and oranges, which were added to the honey cakes. And so *Lebkuchen,* as they are known today, came into being—Nürnberg's first specialty. More than 70 million *Lebkuchen* are baked in that city each year.

Today a number of these simple honey cake bakers still survive in Hungary, kneading honey into flour and pressing the dough into ancient picture molds. A few itinerant bakers shape their cakes into large 12-inch hearts with elaborate icings, pictures, and even tiny mirrors for decoration.

Nürnberger Lebkuchen
(Honey Cookies)

1 cup honey
¾ cup dark brown sugar
1 egg, beaten
1 tbsp. lemon juice
1 tsp. grated lemon peel
2½ cups flour
1 tsp. cinnamon
½ tsp. cloves
½ tsp. cardamom
⅛ tsp. nutmeg
½ tsp. salt
½ tsp. soda
⅓ cup finely chopped candied orange peel and citron
½ cup ground almonds

Heat honey in small pan over medium heat only until it begins to bubble. Do not boil. Remove and cool. Stir in brown sugar, egg, lemon juice, and lemon peel until blended; set aside and cool to lukewarm.

In a large bowl stir together flour (unsifted), spices, salt, and soda. Add honey mixture, candied peel, citron, and almonds, stirring until well blended. Dough will be soft. Cover and refrigerate several days.

On a heavily floured board, roll out a small amount of dough to ⅜-inch thickness. Cut dough in rounds with cutter. Grease baking tin and line with parchment, or place cookies on *Back-*

oblaten.° With fingers, round up cookies toward center. Press almond halves into cookies with half a cherry in center. Bake at 375° 10-12 minutes or until set.

Remove immediately and brush with glaze. If baked on parchment, spread glaze over bottom of cookie as soon as top dries. Store in airtight plastic container; age at least 3 weeks or longer. Makes 20 large cookies.

Lebkuchen dough may also be cut in small heart shapes and topped with Chocolate Glaze.

Glaze I: 1 cup powdered sugar, 5 tbsp. water (or rum).

Glaze II: Boil 1 cup sugar and ½ cup water until first indication of a thread (230°). Remove from heat; stir in ¼ cup powdered sugar. Brush hot icing over cookies. Reheat if necessary. You may also flavor glaze with rosewater.

Chocolate Glaze: 8 oz. semi-sweet chocolate melted over warm water.

° *Backoblaten* (bock-o-blotten) are edible baking discs that keep cookies from sticking to pans. See Shopper's Guide, p. 100.

Zimtsterne
(German Cinnamon Stars)

Cinnamon, a favorite spice at Christmas, enhances these chewy almond stars.

- 2 egg whites
- ⅛ tsp. salt
- 1⅓ cups powdered sugar, sifted
- ½ tsp. lemon juice
- 1 tsp. cinnamon
- 2½ cups + 1 tbsp. ground unblanched almonds

Beat egg whites until stiff. Beat in salt and powdered sugar, 2 tbsp. at a time. The mixture should be stiff and glossy. Beat additionally as necessary so it retains the mark of a knife blade. Set aside ½ cup of whites to coat cookies. Add nuts, cinnamon, and lemon juice. Stir together gently but thoroughly. Mixture should be heavy and fairly solid. Add more almonds if too sticky.

Sprinkle board with sugar and roll dough to ⅜-inch thickness. If dough sticks, sprinkle more sugar on board. Cut dough with small star-shaped cutter. Place on greased baking sheet. Paint each cookie with reserved egg white mixture. Bake at 275° for 20 minutes. Store in airtight container. Makes 2 dozen.

German Kringel

Hard-cooked egg yolks give this cookie a rich, delicate texture. The word *Kringel* means ring or circle.

- ½ cup butter
- ½ cup sugar
- 1 raw egg yolk
- 3 hard-cooked egg yolks, sieved
- ½ tsp. cardamom (optional)
- Grated peel of 1 lemon
- 2 cups cake flour
- 1 egg white
- Sugar
- ½ cup finely chopped blanched almonds

Beat butter and sugar until creamy. Add raw egg yolk, hard-cooked egg yolks, cardamom, and lemon peel. Mix well. Add sifted cake flour, ½ cup at a time. Mix well. Chill overnight and roll out to ¼-inch thickness on lightly floured board. Cut with 2½ inch doughnut cutter.

Brush tops of *Kringel* with slightly beaten egg white and sprinkle with sugar and almonds. Line baking pan with waxed paper or parchment and set *Kringel* on paper. Bake at 375° for 12-15 minutes or until lightly browned. Cool. Makes about 2 dozen.

Nürnberg's Christmas Market

To visit the Christmas market in Nürnberg, Germany, is to become a child again. Here, in the shadow of the old historic *Frauenkirche*, radiating from a large central créche, are hundreds of little lamplit stalls decked with garlands of evergreen.

Irresistible aromas of sizzling *Bratwurst* served with mustard, horseradish, and German potato salad tempt even the staunchest dieter. Farther on, tantalizing stalls offer burnt sugar almonds, the richest of chocolates, colorful marzipan shaped in a garden array of fruits and vegetables. Nearby, too, is one of the famous *Lebkuchen* bakers with oven-fresh honey cookies for sale.

Mingled with the food is a dazzling array of toys to warm the heart of child and adult alike—beautifully handcrafted dolls, trains, cars, the tiniest of Christmas tree ornaments, brightly painted wooden soldiers, straw stars, wax angels, as well as practical gifts of hand-knit sweaters, mittens, and socks.

There is laughter and music from a children's choir caroling on the steps of the *Frauenkirche*.

An ancient legend has it that once the Christ child, drawn by the glittering lights, children's songs, and the aroma of warm, spicy *Lebkuchen*, came down from heaven to do his Christmas shopping at the fair. Since then it has been called the *Christkindlesmarket* (Christ child's market). Every small Nürnberg child deems it wise to be good in December, since it is the *Christkind* who brings gifts on Christmas Eve—and he just may be at the market anytime, doing his Christmas shopping.

German Spitzbuben

(Little Rogues)

A cookie baker's cookie, *Spitzbuben* are served in many German, Austrian, and Swiss homes at Christmas. Sometimes they are called *Drei Augen* (Three Eyes).

1 cup + 4 tbsp. sweet butter
⅔ cup sugar
2 cups flour
⅛ tsp. cinnamon
Strawberry or raspberry jam or currant jelly
Confectioners' sugar

Beat butter and sugar until creamy. Beat in sifted flour and cinnamon, ½ cup at a time. Shape dough into ball. Wrap in waxed paper and chill overnight.

On lightly floured surface or between waxed or parchment paper, roll dough to ⅛-inch thickness. Cut rounds with 2-inch scalloped cutter. With a plain round cutter, 1 inch smaller, cut a hole in center of *half of the circles* to form top ring.

Another variation of this cookie is to cut out 3 small holes (an inverted pastry tip or screw cap from soft drink bottle works well) in the *top* cookie to form three "eyes."

Place all circles on tins lined with parchment and bake at 350° about 12-15 minutes or until golden brown. Transfer to rack after 1 minute. Dust *top* circles with confectioners' sugar.

Spread about ½ tsp. jelly over each *solid* cookie. Cover with sugared top. Spoon extra dab jelly in opening of each cookie. If storing, fill just before serving. Makes 2 dozen.

There were times during World War II when even a slice of black bread was a luxury in Germany. Consequently, to bake something special for Christmas was nearly impossible. Housewives had to save, beg, or barter for a little extra shortening, flour, or sugar to make even a few cookies or a torte.

Yet, somehow, they did manage to make even those bleak days festive. Magdalena Meyer remembers turning mashed potatoes—with a little almond flavoring and a few nuts— into an ersatz *(substitute) marzipan for a Christmas treat.*

Springerle

Springerle are among Germany's most famous Christmas cookies. The squares are pressed from wooden molds in countless prints. Helen Epp, a rare person to enjoy the diamond anniversary of marriage and homemaking, shares her favorite *Springerle* recipe from her own cookie collection.

4 eggs
2 cups sugar
4 drops oil of anise or
  ¼ tsp. anise extract
½ tsp. baking ammonia*
  or ¼ tsp. baking powder
Grated peel of ½ lemon
4 cups cake flour
4 tsp. anise seed

Beat eggs until thick and lemon-colored. Gradually add sugar and beat until mixture is almost white and thick enough to "ribbon." (This makes finished cookie fine grained.) Add anise flavoring, lemon peel, and ammonia dissolved in 1 tsp. water. Gradually add sifted cake flour. Dough should be very firm. Add a little flour if necessary. Chill at least 2 hours.

Dust wooden molds with cornstarch; tap off excess starch. Turn dough onto lightly floured board and roll to ¼-inch thickness. Press dusted wooden molds into dough, bearing down firmly and evenly to leave clear-cut designs. With a floured knife, cut cookies apart. Place on greased baking sheet sprinkled with anise seed. Cover with tea towel and let stand in cool place overnight or up to 24 hour to dry.

In the morning place in 375° oven to set the design; immediately turn down to 300° and bake for 15 minutes. Remove to racks to cool. For softer cookies, let stand overnight before storing in airtight containers. Age 2-3 weeks before serving. (A slice of apple added to the tin the day before serving will soften cookies.) Makes 6 dozen.

---

*Baking ammonia is available in some European delis. See also Shopper's Guide, p. 100.

Some people think the name Springerle *refers to* Springer, *the German name for the knight in a chess game. Others believe it goes back to pagan times when sacrifices were made to the gods. The poor, having no offering, made token gifts in the form of cookies with animal shapes.*

Hints to Springerle Bakers

Springerle bakers suggest that the shape of the cookie varies, depending on the consistency of the dough, whether it is stiff or soft, and what kind of leavening is used. German bakers used *baking ammonia* or *potash*.

Springerle must dry overnight. Then when placed in the oven, only the top of the cookie expands. Because the bottom of the *Springerle* cannot stretch, it stands on "a kind of foot," explains Magdalena Meyer. She suggests sprinkling cookies lightly with water when they come from the oven.

Use cornstarch to dust the mold; it doesn't stick in the fine lines like flour. *Springerle* baking is best done when there is low humidity.

A Christmas Cookie Loft

"Grandmother made all of her Christmas cookies at the end of October," says Magdalena Meyer. "She tied the cookies in small bags, put them in a pillowcase, and hung them in the attic, high enough, of course, so we grandchildren couldn't reach them. The aging improved the flavor and grandmother's cookies were known to be the most delicious."

"*To celebrate* Christmas, our Greek homes must be sparkling and spotless," explains Katina Scamagas, San Jose, California. "A lot of attention is given to cleanliness and washing clothes. Mothers bake *Christopsomo*, our Greek Christmas bread, and a lot of *Baklava* and *Melomacarona* (p. 54).

"When I was young, the only Christmas tree in the village was at school. We cut our own pine and decorated it with balloons, little ribbons, and spread cotton around like snow.

"Early Christmas morning—about five o'clock—children go caroling. Some are from the school. They are invited in (village people get up early!) and given sweets and money, which often goes for a school project.

"In Greece it's St. Basil, not Santa Claus, who brings the children gifts. For this occasion he wears a red robe, a red cap, black boots, and carries a large sack, much like the American Santa. Gifts are exchanged on January 1, St. Basil's Day. Christmas in Greece is a religious holiday, a time for church and family."

Greek Kourabiedes

This buttery Greek holiday cookie (pronounced koo-rah-be-*eth*-es) is buried in a blizzard of powdered sugar. It is served at weddings and festivals and especially at Christmas, when a clove is placed in each cookie, a reminder of the spices wise men brought to the Christ child.

1 cup sweet butter
⅓ cup powdered sugar
2 egg yolks
½ tsp. almond extract
2 cups + 2 tbsp. flour
½ cup ground almonds, lightly toasted

Cream butter and sugar. Add egg yolks and flavoring and beat well. Gradually add flour and mix. Add almonds. Form into a ball and chill for 1 hour. Shape dough into 1-inch balls or crescents. Place on greased baking sheet. Make slight indentation on top of each round cookie. Bake at 350° 15-20 minutes or until very lightly browned.

Remove from sheet and place warm cookies in shallow pan. Sift powdered sugar over tops generously. (Cookies must have plenty of sugar on top.) Store in airtight container. Makes about 2½ dozen.

Greek Melomacarona

(Honey Dainties)

These tender cookies are glazed with honey and dipped in nuts. Aristea Pettis, San Jose, California, makes these tempting delights every Christmas.

½ cup butter or margarine
1 cup safflower oil
½ cup sugar
½ tsp. grated orange peel
½ tsp. grated lemon peel
1 egg yolk
½ tsp. cinnamon
⅛ tsp. cloves
1 tsp. baking powder
3½ cups flour
½ cup orange juice
Honey Syrup
Sugar/Nut Topping

Beat margarine or butter, oil, and sugar until creamy. Add lemon and orange peel, and egg yolk. (Here Mrs. Pettis adds 1½ tsp. cognac.) Add flour sifted with baking powder, cinnamon, and cloves alternately with orange juice. Mix well. Cover and chill overnight. With about 1 tbsp. dough, form slightly rounded ovals, 2 x 1½ inches.

Place on greased baking sheet and bake at 325° for 25-30 minutes. Cool. Dip in Honey Syrup and sprinkle with Sugar/

Nut Topping. If storing cookies, wait until serving time to glaze.

Honey Syrup: 1 cup sugar, ½ cup water, ½ cup honey, ½ tsp. lemon juice. Bring all ingredients to a boil and boil gently for 5 minutes. Skim off foam. Place cookies on wire rack over waxed paper. Dip cooled cookies in Honey Syrup (keep it warm). Sprinkle with topping mixture.

Sugar/Nut Topping: Mix together ½ cup sugar, 1 cup ground or finely chopped walnuts, and ¼ tsp. cinnamon. Makes 4 dozen.

"Greek families don't give gifts at Christmas. It is a religious day," says Aristea Pettis. "We always had a crèche in the corner of the living room. Some of the animals father carved by hand; others we children stuffed and sewed. . . . There was always caroling the whole week before Christmas, and the baking of Kourabiedes *and other cookies as well as* Christopsomo, *a round Christmas bread decorated with a large cross and walnuts."*

EVERY ITALIAN family has a Christmas *Presepe*—a manger scene—which is often quite elaborate. Mother brought ours out on the first day of *Novena*, nine days before Christmas. Many of the figures were family heirlooms, handed down for generations.

Each year we added something new—a bit of moss, some stones, another figure. Not only did we have the holy family, shepherds, and wise men, but also familiar village people—an old peasant woman bringing a basket of eggs to the Baby Jesus, a farmer with a head of cabbage, a man with a bundle of faggots to keep the *Bambino* warm. Each morning we lit candles and offered prayers at the *Presepe*. Again on Christmas Eve, when the candles were burning, we said our prayers and mother put the tiny *Bambino* in his crib.

Sometimes itinerant pipers—*Xampognari*—coming down from the mountains, go from house to house and play their pastoral carols in front of the *Presepe*. It is a lovely, moving time. St. Francis of Assisi originated the *Presepe* 700 years ago. *(Matilde Oliverio shared holiday customs from her childhood in Naples, Italy, with her Italian language students in San Jose, California.)*

Italian Biscotti

These twice-baked cookies make great coffee dunkers.

3 eggs
1 cup sugar
¾ cup vegetable oil
2 tsp. anise seed
  or 1 tsp. vanilla
3 cups flour
2 tsp. soda
½ tsp. salt
1 cup chopped almonds
  or walnuts

Beat eggs until thick and lemon-colored. Gradually add sugar and beat; add oil. Lightly crush anise seed with mortar and pestle. Add to egg mixture. Sift flour, salt, and soda together and gradually add to egg mixture. Beat until smooth. Add nuts. Turn out onto lightly floured board and shape into flat loaves about ½-inch thick and 2½ inches wide, the length of the baking sheet. Place on greased baking sheets. Bake at 375° for 20 minutes.

Remove from oven; cool 2 minutes and slice into ¾-inch pieces. Lay slices, cut side down, on baking sheets. Bake again at 375° for 10 minutes or until just golden brown. Remove to wire racks and cool. *Biscotti* keep very well in airtight containers. Makes about 4 dozen.

Pizzelle

A holiday favorite in Italian homes, *Pizzelle* are baked in a decorative iron on top of the stove. Lonnie De Vincenzi and several friends bake more than a thousand dozen (!) *Pizzelle* for the Italian-American Heritage Festival in San Jose, California. Loni and her husband co-chair this festal occasion.

2 eggs
0 tbsp. sugar
¼ cup melted butter
½ tsp. vanilla
1 tsp. crushed anise seed or 3 drops oil of anise
1 cup flour

Beat eggs until light. Beat in sugar, cooled melted butter, vanilla, and anise seed. Stir in flour. Heat *Pizzelle* iron until hot. Brush lightly with butter. Add a spoonful of batter and bake 1 minute. Turn iron over and bake until both sides are golden. Using a spatula, transfer cookie to wire rack. Makes 14.

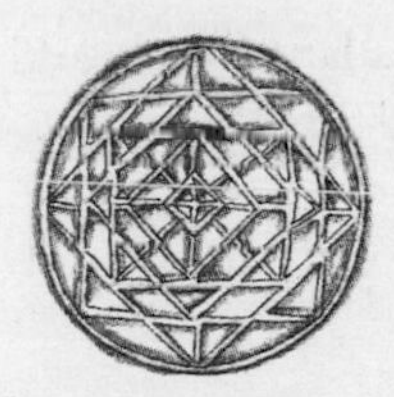

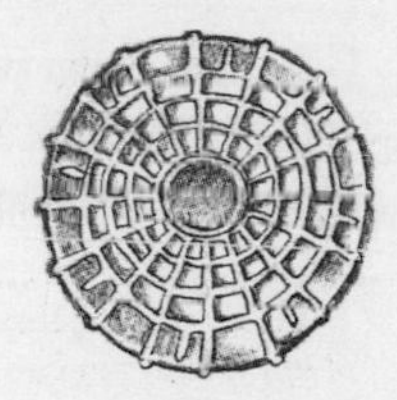

Jeannie Snyder's Cuccidati
(Italian Fig Cookies)

This popular combination of dried fruits, nuts, and pastry came to this country from Sicily. Baked in long rolls and sliced, or tucked into pastry pockets, *Cuccidati* (koo-chi-*da*-ti) are made in many Italian homes and bakeries at Christmas. The recipe comes from Jeannie Bertucelli Snyder, food editor of the Italian/American Heritage paper, in San Jose, California.

Filling

¾ cup each dried figs, prunes, raisins
⅓ cup dates
1 cup glazed fruit cake mix
¾ cup each toasted ground almonds and walnuts
¼ cup chocolate chips (optional)
½ cup water
¼ cup apple juice*
½ cup sugar
¼ tsp. cinnamon
1½ tsp. vanilla

Grind all fruit, fruit cake mix, and nuts into a large bowl. Add chocolate chips (optional), but do *not* grind. In a saucepan, bring to a boil water, sugar, apple juice.

---

*Traditionally, 2 tbsp. EACH of rum and brandy are used for flavoring *in place of apple juice* and are added *after* the sugar syrup.

Add sugar syrup to fruit mixture and let stand overnight. If mixture is dry, add a little more syrup or hot water.

Pastry

2 cups flour	½ cup shortening
2 tsp. baking powder	1 tsp. vanilla
¼ tsp. salt	1 egg, beaten
	4½ tbsp. milk

Sift dry ingredients together and cut in shortening as for pie dough. Combine egg, vanilla, and milk; add to flour and mix lightly into a ball. Divide in half. Roll half of dough into 4 x 18-inch rectangle. Place filling mixture down center of strip. Wet edges of dough with milk. Fold over and seal edges and ends. Make a few slits on top to allow steam to escape. Repeat with remaining pastry and filling. (Thickness of dough should resemble commercial fig newtons.) Please turn page.

Place loaves on greased baking sheet, seam side down. Bake at 325° 25-30 minutes or until golden brown. When cool, slice in 3-inch pieces (or smaller). Glaze each piece with mixture of 1 cup confectioners' sugar and 1½ tbsp. water or milk. Sprinkle with *nonpareil* decorating candies.

Steffani ("Stella") Silva's family has been making Cuccidati *from the same Sicilian recipe for more than a hundred years. "Grandmother made her fruit squares rather large, decorating them with designs of pastry dough—pyrocantha wreaths, birds in a nest, Christmas trees, or fish, cutting tiny scales with a scissors. Because* Cuccidati *are rich, I prefer to make my squares smaller—just bite size," she says.*

Mrs. Silva's grandmother added orange to her recipe. Baking the orange before grinding gave the filling a lovely, unique flavor.

Steffani Silva's Cuccidati
(Italian Fig Cookies)

Filling

- ⅔ cup dried apricots
- 1 cup or 8 oz. dates
- 1½ cups raisins
- 1 12-oz. pkg dried white figs
- 1 cup glazed fruit cake mix
- ½ large orange
- 1 cup chopped nuts
- 1 cup honey
- ½ tsp. each nutmeg. cinnamon, cloves, black pepper (optional) and vanilla
- ½ tsp. rum extract (optional)

Dice apricots and fruit cake mix; set aside. Grind dried fruits and orange with rind into large bowl. Add apricots, fruit cake mix, nuts, honey, spices, and flavorings. Mix well. Soften filling with hot water; add sugar only to taste. Let stand overnight.

To finish *Cuccidati*, follow pastry, glazing, and decorating directions, pp. 61 and 62. Double pastry recipe. Makes 4 18-inch loaves. Slice in 1-inch pieces or larger.

IN THE SMALL Italian village where Angela Gagliardi grew up, St. Barbara's Day has special meaning. Barbara not only is the patron saint of Piane Crati, but the village church bears her name as well.

Each year on December 4, the women of Piane Crati celebrate *Pitanza* with a feast table laden with breads and pastries in honor of their saint, who as a young girl, disobeyed her father's wishes and shared grain with the poor. Village people go from house to house saying, "*Pitanza*!" meaning "Give me a pittance." No one is refused on this day.

Ever since Mrs. Gagliardi came to this country she has kept this village tradition with an open house on St. Barbara's Day. At 82, she still bakes a wide array of her native Calabrian delicacies and invites more than 100 friends to her special *Pitanza* in her San Jose, California, home. No one is turned away. Before leaving, each guest is given a tiny replica of St. Barbara's hands which Mrs. Gagliardi fashions out of *Tarali* dough.

One year Angela was hospitalized on the feast day. This posed a real problem: Never had she broken her tradition! But thanks to family and friends who brought a *portable Pitanza*, Angela kept the custom—even in her hospital room. And no one was turned away.

Angela Gagliardi vows that as long as she is able, her home will be open to celebrate the Feast of *Pitanza* every December 4.

MEXICO contributes many colorful traditions to the Christmas celebration, but perhaps the most loved by children is the breaking of the *Piñata* on Christmas Eve.

Bought at the marketplace or made at home, *Piñatas* are big earthenware jars decorated with cardboard and brightly colored tissue paper in the shapes of animals, flowers, or huge paper stars.

Oranges, bananas, tangerines, peanuts, and pieces of sugarcane are stuffed into the jar which is suspended from a rope so it may be pulled up and down. Each child is blindfolded, given a stick, spun in a circle, and told to swing at the *Piñata*. If he swishes the air near the guests, everyone shrieks with fear and laughter. When at last someone cracks the jar, the children scramble to pick up their treats. Extra baskets of tropical fruits are shared by the hostess with the rest of her guests.

Originating in Italy, the *Piñata* tradition came to Spain where it took on religious significance during the Lenten season. In Mexico it is part of the Christmas *Posada* celebration.

THE BIGGEST event in our village in Mexico was the Christmas *Posada* (meaning inn), remembers Rosa Calvillo, Milpitas, California. When I was a little girl, everyone in the parish was invited. For nine evenings we went to nine different homes. Two children, carrying images of Mary and Joseph, led the candlelight procession around the house, singing traditional songs and asking for shelter. Each time the innkeeper replied, "No room!"

After being turned away several times, we were finally welcomed at the last door on which they knocked. The procession entered the house and we placed our lighted candles around the *Nacimiento* (crèche). After the religious ceremony, there was a *Piñata* for the children. On Christmas Eve we celebrated with *Tamales, Buñuelos,* hot chocolate, and candy-covered almonds.

"The next morning we got up early and went to sunrise mass. It was a big thrill to see the beautiful nativity scene where the Baby Jesus had been laid. We lined up to go by the crèche to make sure he was there!"

Mexican Buñuelos

(Fried Sweet Fritters)

Crisp, fluffy rounds, sprinkled with cinnamon and sugar, make a perfect complement to mugs of frothy hot chocolate on Christmas Eve. *Buñuelos* (boo-ny*ue*-los) are traditional among Mexican people, wherever they live.

4 eggs	1 tsp. baking powder
¼ cup sugar	1 tsp. salt
1 tsp. vegetable oil	1 cup sugar
2 cups flour	1 tsp. cinnamon

In a bowl, combine eggs and sugar and beat until thick and lemon-colored. Add oil. Combine 1½ cups unsifted flour, baking powder, and salt, and gradually add to eggs. Beat well. Turn dough onto board, using remaining flour. Knead until smooth and elastic.

Shape dough into 16 balls. Roll each ball into a 5-inch circle. Lay on waxed paper, uncovered, about 10 minutes. Fry in deep hot oil at 350° until golden brown, turning once. Drain on paper towels. Sprinkle with cinnamon/sugar mixture. Store in airtight container.

There is much laughter and good fun while making Buñuelos *in Rosa Calvillo's home on Christmas Eve. Rosa "calls out the troops" and rounds up everyone—uncles, aunts, grandmothers, children—to help roll out their* Buñuelos *(p. 68). "Everyone works, even if it means rolling the dough on a cloth on your lap. I like it because it brings my whole family together," she says.*

Good food and good Buñuelos *are traditions Rosa adopted from her grandmother, Aurora Larriva, a fine cook who sold* Tacos, Burritos, *and* Tortas *from a small sidewalk vending stand in the little Mexican village of Torreon (Coahuila). "Grandmother was always making something special. That's where I learned to cook."*

Biscochitos

"*Biscochitos* are Spanish," explains Lodean Phillips, who makes them in her Los Alamos, New Mexico, home. "They are traditional at Christmas and are used for weddings and feast days. I've also eaten them on feast days of Indian friends in their pueblo homes.... *Biscochitos* are crisp and lightly flavored with anise—a cookie that is very easy to eat."

½ cup sugar
1 cup lard
1 egg, beaten
½ tsp. anise extract
1½ tsp. crushed anise seed
1½ tsp. baking powder
½ tsp. salt
3½ tbsp. orange juice
3½ cups flour
Cinnamon-sugar topping

Cream lard. Add sugar, egg, extract, anise seed; beat well. Sift baking powder, flour, and salt. Add gradually to first mixture. Add orange juice and blend. Chill overnight. Roll ⅛-inch thick and cut into shapes. Dip top of each cookie in mixture of ¼ cup sugar and ½ tsp. cinnamon. Place on greased baking sheet. Bake at 375° for 5-7 minutes or just until edges turn golden brown. Watch closely. Cool.

IN POLISH farm homes sheaves of grain, brought into the house on Christmas Eve, are tied with colored ribbons and placed in corners of the room. Prayers are said for a bountiful harvest. Grain, a good crop, and harvest all intertwine with the Christmas festival.

Polish women, even now, put fresh clean straw under the Christmas tablecloth, a reminder of the manger in Bethlehem.

"In Serbian homes they used to scatter straw around the whole house," relates Dusanka Tkachenko, "but now in America, it's mainly done in the churches (Serbian)."

She recalled, too, the earlier yule log ceremony when the mother threw a handful of wheat over the log as it was brought in. The father announced, "Christ is born!" And the family replied, "Indeed, he is born!"

Sometimes the whole family formed a procession behind the mother, going from room to room, covering floors with straw. In the kitchen they gathered around a box of wheat with a tall lighted candle while the father prayed for health, happiness, and good crops in the coming year. After this came the Christmas Eve supper.

Polish Poppy Seed Cookies

Poppy seeds are a favorite in Polish Christmas baking. Here is a simple combination of a delicate butter cookie and a crunchy poppy seed topping.

1 cup butter	2 raw egg yolks
¾ cup sugar	2 cups flour
1 tsp. vanilla	½ tsp. salt
2 hard-cooked egg yolks, sieved	Egg White Glaze
	Poppy seeds

Beat butter, sugar, and vanilla until creamy. Add sieved egg yolks and raw egg yolks to sugar and mix well. Add sifted flour and salt gradually. Chill dough. Roll out small portions to ¼-inch thickness on floured board. Cut in 1½-2-inch rounds. Place on greased baking sheet. Brush with 1 egg white beaten with 1 tbsp. water. Sprinkle with poppy seeds. Bake at 350° for 10-12 minutes or until delicately browned. Makes about 3 dozen.

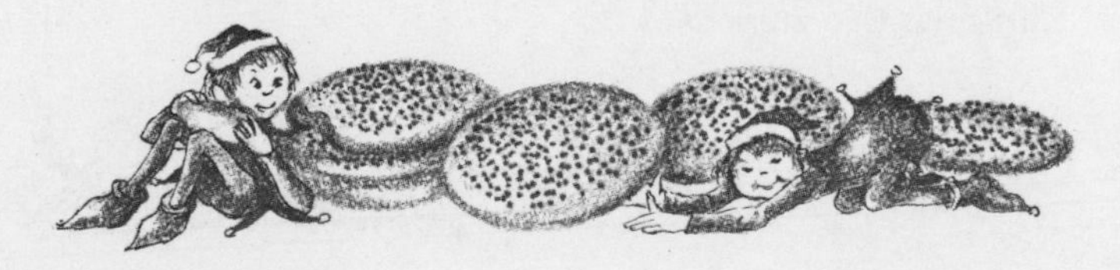

Rumanian Pine Nut Macaroons

Toasted pine nuts accent these airy almond-filled macaroons.

- 2 egg whites
- ⅛ tsp. cream of tartar
- ⅔ cup powdered sugar
- ⅓ cup sugar
- ¼ tsp. almond extract
- 1½ cups ground toasted almonds
- 1¼ oz. pine nuts, slightly toasted
- ¼ cup sugar

Beat egg whites with cream of tartar until foamy. Add sugar gradually; add almond extract and beat until very stiff. Gently fold in almonds. Cover cookie sheet with parchment. Drop meringue mixture by teaspoonfuls over a few pine nuts. Sprinkle tops of meringues with remaining pine nuts and granulated sugar.

Bake at 350° for 15 minutes or until golden brown. Cool and store in airtight container. Makes 3 dozen.

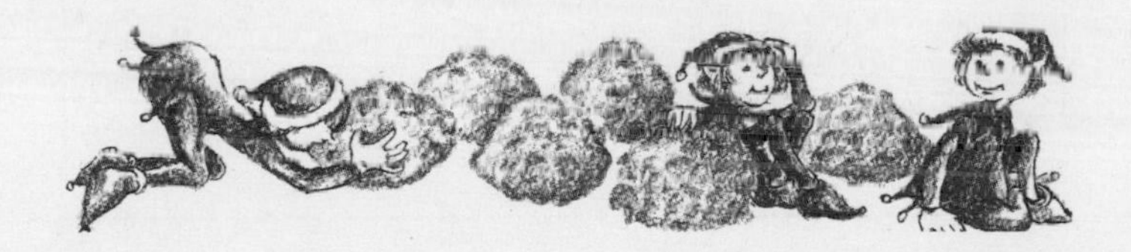

Danish
Christmas Eve Supper

RISENGRÖD (Rice Porridge)

GAASESTEG MED AEBLER OG SVESKER
(Roast Goose with Apples and Prunes)

RØDKAAL (Red Cabbage)

BRUNEDE KARTOFLER (Browned Potatoes)

KAFFEE (Coffee)

AEBLEKAGE, JULEKAGE
(Apple Cake, Christmas Cake)

LIKÖRER (Liqueurs)

THERE IS AN old saying in Denmark that the spirit of Christmas must not leave the house. Danish housewives capture the spirit by offering Christmas baking to everyone who comes to the door.

Early in December they bake hundreds of cookies. Family recipes may yield ten dozen or more and it is not unusual for some women to turn out 300 *Brune Kager* (brown cakes). Cookie batters are stirred early so flavors and spices mingle before baking.

A final test of good Danish cookies is crispness. Butter helps, and so does careful rolling, they say. But there is still another ingredient in Scandinavian recipes that makes their cookies lighter and thinner—*salt of hartshorn,* or baking ammonia *(ammonium bicarbonata).* For instance, in Karen Berg's little book, *Danish Home Baking,* most of the cookie recipes call for *salt of hartshorn.*

Baking ammonia predates baking powder and once was made from the antlers of a deer. Now it is produced chemically. The aroma is potent, but when baked, there is not a trace. Results are worth the slight discomfort. Baking ammonia is available in many European delicatessens. (See also p. 100.)

Finskbröd

(Finnish Shortbread)

Baked in Denmark and throughout Scandinavia, Finnish shortbread is a popular light, buttery cookie made for the Christmas holiday.

1 cup sifted flour
¼ cup sugar
½ cup ground almonds
½ cup butter
1 egg white
¼ cup finely chopped almonds
2 tbsp. sugar

In a mixing bowl, combine flour, sugar, and ground almonds. Cut in butter and mix into a soft dough. Wrap and chill 15 minutes. Roll dough into ½-inch ropes, laying ropes parallel to each other. With a sharp knife, cut across in 2-inch pieces. Brush with beaten egg white. Dip each piece in a mixture of chopped almonds and sugar.

Place cookies slightly apart on greased baking sheet. Bake at 350° about 15 minutes or until golden brown. Cool on cookie sheet and remove carefully. Makes about 4½ dozen.

Berliner Kranser

(Berlin Wreaths)

Liz Nelson, Los Gatos, California, offers this Norwegian favorite on her holiday cookie trays. "I decorate my wreaths with bits of red and green cherries, but my (Norwegian) mother doesn't think that's right at all!"

1 cup butter
½ cup sugar
2 raw egg yolks
2 hard-cooked egg yolks, sieved
¼ tsp. each lemon and orange extract
½ tsp. vanilla*
2½ cups flour

Beat butter and sugar until creamy. Stir in raw and hard-cooked egg yolks and flavoring. Add flour and mix until smoothly blended. Chill briefly. Cut off small amounts of dough and roll in pencil-thin strips. Form a circle and loop one end over and through. Brush wreaths with 1 egg beaten with 1 tbsp. water and dip in coarse (crushed loaf) sugar.

Place on greased baking sheet and bake at 350° for 12-15 minutes or until golden brown. Remove immediately. Makes 5 dozen.

---

*Alternate flavoring: ½ tsp. almond extract *only*. Top wreath with mixture of sugar and ground almonds.

"My mother always made *Fattigman* for Christmas. She stored them in airtight containers in the coolest place in the house—on the steps leading to the attic, which was quite cold in our Minnesota home," says Muriel Schlichting of San Jose, California. "*Fattigman* stay fresh a long time that way."

° ° °

"My mother, who is now 84, still bakes *Klenor* (the Swedish version of *Fattigman)* every Christmas, but not in such big quantities as before," writes Dr. Ingrid Gamstorp of Uppsala. "*Klenor* are often served with berries, preferably raspberries and whipped cream, as a dessert, perhaps together with a glass of port wine."

° ° °

Fattigmans Bakkels, Norwegian crullers dusted with powdered sugar, are known in Sweden as *Klenor*, in Denmark as *Klenje,* and the Finns call them *Klenetit,* all meaning small or little.

Fattigmans Bakkels

In Norwegian, *Fattigmans Bakkels* means poor man's baked goods. Not anymore! But they are well worth the price and effort.

- 4 egg yolks
- ⅓ cup sugar
- ½ tsp. grated lemon peel
- ¼ cup whipping cream
- ½ tsp. cardamom
- 1½ cups flour

Beat egg yolks, sugar, and lemon peel until very thick. (Traditionally, 1 tbsp. brandy is added to the mixture to cut the grease.) Add cream slowly, mixing well. Sift flour and cardamom; add gradually to eggs. Wrap dough and chill overnight. Heat oil (Scandinavian bakers insist lard gives *Fattigman* a better flavor) to 365° or 370°.

Roll dough 1/16-inch thick on floured surface or between sheets of waxed paper. With a pastry wheel cut in diamond shapes, 3 x 2 inches wide. Make lengthwise slit down center of each and tuck under and pull through. Handle dough lightly. Fry to golden brown; turn. Drain on paper towels. Cool. Sprinkle with confectioners' sugar. Store in airtight containers.

Norwegian Sandbakkelser

Liz Nelson grew up in a Norwegian-American home, studies Norwegian, and is active in Sons of Norway. "Norwegians usually serve these tart shells plain, like a cookie," says Liz. Her shells are especially light and flaky.

In Sweden they add ground almonds to the dough and call the tarts *Mandelmusslor*. Both Danes and Swedes may fill the shells with frozen raspberries and whipped cream, raspberry jam, or even a buttercream.

1 cup butter	½ tsp. cardamom
1 cup lard	½ tsp. vanilla
1½ cups sugar	¼ tsp. almond extract
2 eggs	4 cups flour

Beat butter, lard, and sugar until creamy. Add eggs, one at a time, beating well. Add cardamom, vanilla, and almond. Gradually add sifted flour and knead well. Chill overnight. Press walnut-sized pieces of dough evenly around bottom and sides of *Sandbakkelse* tins.

Bake shells on ungreased baking sheet at 350° for 8-10 minutes. Cool completely in tins. Turn over and tap gently to release. Makes 4 dozen.

STRICTLY FOR the birds! Before sitting down to Christmas dinner, the farmers in Scandinavian countries give the birds their Yuletide feast. The finest sheaf of oats or wheat, saved from the summer's harvest, is put on a pole on top of the barn. This custom is followed in many Scandinavian-American communities.

Ester Harvest, a Danish-American, emphasizes, "It wouldn't be Christmas unless the birds are taken care of!"

Ruth Yoder's Perfect Krumkake

Baked on traditional irons engraved with Christmas or decorative scenes, these crisp cookies, rolled into cone shapes, may be eaten plain or filled with whipped cream and fruit.

Ruth's family recipe comes from her grandmother, Ingaborg Hjertass, who lived in Oslo. "Every Norwegian to whom I've given this recipe likes it and uses it," says Ruth.

1½ cups flour
½ cup cornstarch
¾ cup melted butter
1¼ cups sugar
4 eggs
1 tsp. fresh ground cardamom
1 cup whipping cream

Sift flour and cornstarch together; set aside. Melt butter over double boiler. Add sugar to butter. Cool. With spatula or wooden spoon, beat in eggs, 1 at a time. Add cardamom.

Beginning with ⅓ cup cream, alternate flour and cream in small amounts, using downward motion to "pull in the flour." Slowly warm seasoned 5-6-inch *Krumkake* iron over medium heat (about 10-15 minutes). Brush with melted butter.

For each cookie spoon about 1 iced teaspoon batter into center of iron; close. Bake over gas flame or electric burner about 20 seconds first side; 30 second second side. (Timing depends on your stove.)

Remove hot cookie, leave flat, shape into a cone, or roll into a cylinder with wooden *Krumkake* form (available in kitchenware shops) or inside a glass. Cool on seam on rack. Serve plain or filled with whipped cream and fruit. Makes 75.

Swedish Pepparkakor

Pepparkakor are made in every Swedish home at Christmas. Earlier ginger and pepper were used interchangeably; therefore the pepper prefix for this ginger-flavored cookie.

The original recipe for this cookie, using only ginger as the flavoring, was brought from Sweden by Edith Carlson to her new home in Lindsborg, Kansas, many years ago. It was used to make the *Pepparkakor* for Lindsborg's first *Hyllningsfest* (pioneer festival) in 1941.

½ cup sugar
½ cup light molasses
½ cup butter
1 tsp. ginger
½ tsp. cinnamon
½ tsp. mace or nutmeg
¼ tsp. cloves
1 tbsp. grated orange peel
1½ tsp. soda
1 egg, beaten
2 cups flour
¼ tsp. salt

Combine first 8 ingredients in a saucepan over low heat; bring to a boil, remove from heat and stir in soda. Cool to lukewarm and add egg. Gradually mix in sifted flour and salt. (Dough is quite soft.) Chill overnight. Roll out 1/16-inch thick, using as little flour as possible on pastry board. Cut in shapes of hearts, stars, roosters, reindeer.

Place on greased baking sheet and bake at 375° for 5-7 minutes or until cookies are golden brown. Cool on pans. Outline edges of cookies with Royal Icing. Makes 7 dozen 2-inch cookies.

Royal Icing: Beat at high speed 1 egg white with ⅛ tsp. cream of tartar and dash of salt for 1 minute. Add 2 cups sifted powdered sugar. Beat slowly until blended. At high speed beat until very stiff (3-5 minutes). Press through decorating tube with plain tip. Allow frosting to dry before storing.

A Swedish Pepparkakor *tree is topped with a sheaf of wheat The wooden rods are tipped with bright red apples and frosted* Pepparkakor *are hung from the wooden branches.*

AFTER ST. LUCIA'S DAY (December 13) cookie baking begins in earnest in Scandinavian homes.

In earlier times, housewives used to get up as early as 4:00 in the morning, tiptoe down to their cold kitchens, and begin mixing their Christmas cookies. An old superstition had it that no sunlight should shine on the dough or disaster would befall the household. Every housewife hoped for a crescent moon lingering on the horizon to bring good luck to her baking.

Housewives still love to outdo each other, making hundreds and hundreds of cookies of many varieties. Formerly they were packed in tightly covered tins until the afternoon of the 24th when, according to tradition, folks were allowed to taste them for the first time.

Before going to church on Christmas, mothers frequently set out piles of goodies for each member of the family. And children ate to their heart's content when they returned home after the service.

Christmas baking is enjoyed especially after Christmas Day when there is more time to sit and chat, sip coffee, and eat the Christmas cookies and cakes.

Swedish Spritz

A Christmas favorite in Scandinavia, these buttery *Spritz* are a wonderful time saver in a busy season.

1 cup butter
⅔ cup sugar
3 egg yolks

1 tsp. almond extract
⅓ tsp. cream of tartar
⅛ tsp. salt
2½ cups flour

Beat butter and sugar together until creamy. Add egg yolks and almond extract and mix well. Sift together flour, cream of tartar, and salt. Gradually add to creamed mixture, mixing until smooth. Pack dough into a cookie tube press and shape dough in circles or S's on greased baking sheet.

Using the thin, flat wafer cutout, press long strips of dough onto greased baking sheets. Bake at 350° for 8-10 minutes or until edges of cookies are golden brown. With sharp knife, cut diagonally across strips, making 2½-inch cookies. Remove and cool on racks. Makes 5 dozen wafers or 40-50 shaped cookies.

TALES OF TROLLS and goblins have long been part of Nordic lore, passed on by grandmothers from one generation to the next. In Denmark, the *Julnisse* (Christmas elves) are said to live in every barn, protecting house and animals from harm. The Swedes' lovable *Tomte* is a cross between an Irish leprechaun and the Dutch St. Nicholas. A pointed cap and flowing white beard identify the *Julnisse* of Norway.

If not treated properly, the story goes, these little pranksters will mix up milk buckets, tangle horses' manes, and even make cows sick. So it is traditional at Christmas for the Scandinavians to reward their *Nisse* with a bowlful of rice for his faithful protection.

Thyra Bjorn writes, "Even as we outgrew many of these superstitions, it was still hard to realize that our beloved *Tomte* was a myth and that he did not really eat the big bowlful of rice porridge we set on the step on Christmas Eve."*

Today this tradition is kept mainly by grandparents for the sake of their children.

---

*Thyra Ferre Bjorn, *Once upon a Christmas Time* (New York, N.Y.: Holt, Rinehart, Winston).

A Scotch Hogmanay Supper

(New Year's Eve)

KIPPER CREAM
(Kippered Herring in Cream Sauce)

AYRSHIRE BACON OR HAM

SALADS

BLACK BUN
(Fruit/Nut Filling in a Pastry Shell)

SHORTBREAD

Scotch Shortbread

In Scotland, shortbread is traditionally made only for New Year's Eve. Doreen Leith, a native of Glasgow, makes hers in a 6-inch circle. When it comes from the oven, she sprinkles it with sugar and quickly scores it into 16 wedges. When cool, it is broken, rather than cut, for good luck.

Doreen's mother says, "Good shortbread requires cold butter and cold hands so the oil won't run in the butter." The dough may be soft, but not sticky.

½ cup sweet butter	1 cup flour
¼ cup superfine sugar	½ cup rice flour*

Cream butter and sugar. Sift flours together. Work into butter mixture until smooth; form into a ball. Chill. Pat dough into 6 or 7-inch circle. Flute edges. Place on pan lined with waxed paper. Bake at 325° for 40-45 minutes or until golden brown and done in the center.

Using a knife, score into 16 triangles; sprinkle lightly with sugar while hot. Cool on rack. Break into pieces for serving. Makes 1 shortbread.

*Available in health food stores.

Lang May Yur Lum Reek!

The celebration of *Hogmanay,* or New Year, belongs most truly to the Scots.

Though the origin of the word is lost, the custom derives from the good fairy of Norse folklore. At midnight the menfolk set out to "first-foot" neighbors and friends—the first man to cross the threshold of a home in the New Year is the first-foot.

Traditionally, a first-foot brings with him a piece of coal, a bottle of Scotch, and a piece of bread or a thin oat cake. The lump of coal is shared with the rousing wish, "Lang may yur lum reek!" (Long may your chimney smoke!) "A wee dram of Scotch" is said to bring the friend good luck, and bread expresses the hope they may be well provided for.

Doreen Leith's father, Ernest LeSage, had first-footed a dear friend for more than 40 years. When the Leith's second child was born, Doreen's father delayed a visit to see his new grandson because it was *Hogmanay.* His friend, who was ill, had requested that Mr. LeSage first-foot him, as he had for so long. It was important to her father to remain in Glasgow to carry on this tradition—and welcome his new grandson later.

"In our home we first-foot, too," Doreen relates. "We always have a big *Hogmanay* party, and at midnight, my husband,

David, goes outside and knocks. I answer the door. He wishes everyone a good New Year—sometimes he brings with him chocolates or bread. . . . A first-footer should be tall, dark, and handsome, for good luck, and David fits all three."

First-footing is carried on into January. It also has significance for the first time you visit someone's home. "My mother always took a gift, a plant, some heather, or some small thing whenever she made a first visit to another home." *(Doreen Leith is a teacher and lives in Palo Alto, California.)*

Basler Leckerli

- ¾ cup good quality honey
- 1 cup sugar
- 3 tbsp. lemon juice*
- 2 cups finely chopped almonds
- ⅔ cup chopped candied orange and lemon peel
- Grated peel of ½ lemon
- 4 tsp. cinnamon
- 1 tsp. nutmeg
- ½ tsp. cloves
- 1 tsp. baking powder
- 3 cups flour
- Leckerli Glaze

Melt honey in a large saucepan (not over 122° F); do not boil. Remove from heat. Add sugar and lemon juice and stir until dissolved. Cool to lukewarm. Gradually add ¾ of the flour sifted with spices and baking powder. Mix well. Add remaining ingredients. Turn out onto board with remaining flour and knead it into the dough. Dough will be stiff. Cover tightly and chill for several days.

Bring dough to room temperature. On floured board, roll dough to fit 10 x 14-inch tin. Place in greased and floured baking pan. Bake at 350° for about 30 minutes or until done. Brush

*Most Swiss recipes use Kirsch in place of lemon juice for tenderness. If using Kirsch, omit baking powder.

off excess flour. Brush with glaze while still hot. Cool and cut into 2 x 3-inch rectangles. Store in airtight container several weeks before serving.

Leckerli Glaze: 1 cup powdered sugar mixed with 3 tbsp. lemon juice.

Basler Leckerli

Basel, the old Swiss city along the Rhine, boasts this specialty which goes back 500 years. With minor exceptions, these spicy honey cookies remain much the same today as those made by the proud Basel burghers back in the fifteenth century.

During the Christmas season, these famous confections are baked in every home and sold in markets and bakeries all over Switzerland. Irvine Nussbaumer, who manages Migros bakeries in Basel and Tesin, says they bake from three to four tons of *Leckerli* every week during Christmas. Mr. Nussbaumer notes that the quality of honey used is important—get the best, and one low in sugar content.

My introduction to *Leckerli* (meaning delicious) was in the home of Erna Würgler many Christmases ago in Basel. Erna's recipe (page 94) comes from her baker husband, Jacques. *Leckerli,* like good friendships, improve with age.

Sablés

Topped with tangy lemon glaze, *Sablés* (meaning sand or dry cake) are the ultimate in delectable butter cookies. This delicacy is part of the baking repertoire of Lilly Gyger, who bakes Swiss cakes and tortes for a homey little restaurant at Bienenberg, overlooking the village of Liestal, Switzerland.

½ cup + 3½ tbsp. sweet butter
⅓ cup + 1½ tsp. sugar
½ tsp. salt
1 tsp. vanilla or ½ pkg. vanilla sugar
2 cups flour
Lemon Glaze

Cream butter. Add sugar and beat until creamy. Add vanilla and salt. Add sifted flour gradually. Mix well. Shape into a 2-inch round roll. Wrap in plastic or waxed paper. Chill overnight. Cut in thin slices. Bake on greased baking sheet. Bake at 350° for 8-10 minutes or until golden brown around the edges. Remove from pan. Glaze while hot. Makes about 3 dozen.

Lemon Glaze: Mix together ½ cup powdered sugar and 3 tsp. lemon juice.

Basler Brunsli

Another unique specialty of good bakers in Switzerland is this chocolate-almond, macaroon-meringue cookie. Liesel Widmer, a staff member of the Mennonite Bible school in Liestal, Switzerland, shared this recipe.

4 egg whites
1 cup powdered sugar
1 cup granulated sugar
1 cup ground almonds
1 cup ground filberts
1 tsp. cinnamon
½ tsp. cloves
3 oz. unsweetened baking chocolate, ground

In a large mixing bowl, combine ground nuts and chocolate. Set aside. Beat egg whites until foamy. Gradually beat in sugar. Add cinnamon and cloves. Beat until mixture is stiff. Gently fold egg whites into almond-chocolate mixture.

Spread about ⅓ cup sugar on a large board. Sprinkle 2 tbsp. sugar on the top. Roll dough to ¼-inch thickness. Use additional sugar if necessary.

Cut with small shaped cutters or slice into 1 x 2-inch bars. Place on foil or parchment-lined cookie sheet. Bake at 325° for about 15-20 minutes or until dry. Do not overbake. Makes about 4 dozen small cookies.

Hanni Roth's Mandelmailänderli

(Little almond cookies from Milan)

1 cup + 2 tbsp. butter
½ cup sugar
2 eggs
Grated rind of
½ lemon
1¼ cups ground
unblanched almonds
2 cups flour
Egg Glaze

Beat butter and sugar until light and creamy. Add eggs, beating well. Add lemon rind and almonds. Gradually add sifted flour, blending well. Chill dough overnight. On floured surface or between sheets of waxed paper, roll small amounts of dough to ⅛-inch thickness. Keep dough chilled. Cut designs with floured cutter. (Swiss women use *Mailänderli* cutters, 1¼-inch in diameter in shapes of hearts, stars, crescents.)

Place cookies on greased baking sheet. Brush cookies with glaze of 1 egg yolk beaten with 1 tbsp. water. Sprinkle with granulated sugar. Bake at 350° for 10-12 minutes or until golden brown around the edges. Cool on racks.

From late November on, Hanni Roth's Basel kitchen is filled with the marvelous aromas of cinnamon, anise, nutmeg, and vanilla sugar. On Advent Sundays she entertains around the lighted candles of their Advent wreath. Her home is always open to foreign guests.

It was on such a Sunday we sat together singing carols in English and German and talking of the delights of Swiss Christmas baking. Since then, *Mailänderli* have been a family favorite.

Mailänderli supposedly come from Milan, but people there are not familiar with the cookie. When you try them, you'll know what they miss!

Shopper's Guide

Backoblaten: Available in some European delicatessens.

Chestnut Puree: Imported from France, available in some import stores and specialty groceries.

Baker's Ammonia, Coating Chocolate and Paramount Crystals: Available in many cake decorating supply shops. Mail order from:

Maid of Scandinavia
3244 Raleigh Ave.
Minneapolis, MN 55416

Oil of Anise: Local pharmacies.

Rose and Orange Water: Both may be found in Greek and Middle Eastern delicatessens, some liquor stores. Order by mail from:

International Delicatessen
789 The Alameda
San Jose, CA 95126

SPECIAL COOKIE CUTTERS, IRONS, AND MOLDS

Fattigman Cutters, Decorating Tubes and Pastry Sets, Wooden Krumkake Forms, and Sandbakkelser Tins: Available in some Scandinavian import shops. Order by mail from:

Maid of Scandinavia
3244 Raleigh Ave.
Minneapolis, MN 55416

Krumkake irons, Pizzelle irons, and all forms of cookie cutters. Buy in gourmet cookware shops or order by mail from:

Maid of Scandinavia
3244 Raleigh Ave.
Minneapolis, MN 55416

Speculaas molds. Sometimes found in Dutch bakeries or gift shops. Order by mail from:

Maid of Scandinavia
3244 Raleigh Ave.
Minneapolis, MN 55416

Holland Pastry & Gift Shop
524 S. Bascom
San Jose, CA 95128

Custom-made cookie cutters by tinsmiths.
Order by mail from:

Stained glass cutter
(see recipe, p. 18)
Eugene Valasek
4518 17th St. NW
Canton, OH 44708

Niels Larsen
624 E. Dennison St.
Appleton, WI 54011

Little Fox Factory
931 Marion Rd.
Bucyrus, OH 44820

Handcarved wooden cookie molds (initialed, dated, numbered) and catalogs available from:

Gene Wilson
HOBI Handcrafts
P.O. Box 25
Belleville, IL 62222

D. D. Dillon Carvings
850 Meadow Lane
Camp Hill, PA 17011

Cookie Cutter Collector's Club. For information write:

Cookie Cutter Collector's Club
5426 27th St., N.W.
Washington, DC 20015

Christmas Cookie Index

Dear Reader,

As you browse through this book, may you, too, come to appreciate the beauty of Christmases past.

Without exception, the women who shared memories of Christmases in other lands, spoke with a nostalgia, a fondness, almost a reverence as they recalled the traditions, the baking, the family rituals handed down to them through many generations.

Whatever your heritage—learn about it. Talk with your grandparents, great uncles and aunts, about their early Christmas traditions—especially if they lived in another country. From them you will gain a better understanding of your family and the heritage which is yours.

And if possible, pass on to your children in some tangible way the beauty, security, and warmth that come from preserving those Christmas traditions of the past.

Norma Jost Voth
San Jose, California